The Instagram Creative Brand Guide

Copyright © 2023 Sincere Chinenye Igwilo
All rights reserved.
ISBN: 9798391113737

TABLE OF CONTENT

What is Branding all About?	Pg 1
How to Build a Brand as a Creative?	Pg 3
How to Rebrand Your Page?	Pg 14
How to Build a Valuable Brand?	Pg 18
How to Build a Consistent Brand?	Pg 21
Content Calendar, Repurposing & Scheduling	Pg 32
How to Monetize Your Brand?	Pg 39
Content Strategy	Pg 46

ABOUT ME

Igwilo Chinenye Sincere

Content writer, Instagram creative consultant

Igwilo Chinenye Sincere is a Content writer/storyteller, Instagram creative brand coach, a social media & community manager.

In this EBook, you will find out how to Brand your Instagram page as a creative with strategies that actually work simplified to the simplest form using my experience and examples as benchmarks.

let's be friends

CONTENTS

1. What is branding all about

2. How to build a brand as a creative

I. What is your brand about?
II. Who is your brand for?
III. Where to find them?
IV. How to get them? (Engagement Strategy)
V. How to keep them? (Community building)

3. How to rebrand your page

4. How to build a valuable brand

5. How to build a consistent brand

I. Content Calendar
II. Content Repurposing
III. Content Scheduling

6. How to monetize your brand

BONUS CHAPTER

7. Content strategy

I. Content Format
II. Content Type
III Content

WHAT IS BRANDING ALL ABOUT?

Branding is what I call "packaging". It is how you position and arrange your brand to be perceived by others, what distinguishes your brand from that of another, and what makes others recognize you, it is your IDENTITY.

Branding is more than a logo, a color, or a font. It doesn't mean that these things aren't important because let's take for example; if I see a black &white background video, I'm thinking, "This is Salem king", if I see a tweet with a pink animation profile picture, I'm thinking "its Phoenix blvck" if I see a particular carousel design & color "I'm thinking Chisom Nnaji".

But before I became aware of their logo, color, or design, it was what I knew them for, what I knew I was going to get from them, it was their content that kept me long enough to remember their logo, color, or design.

Some people's logos are their faces or their name. What would make you remember the name or face of someone you may not physically know? They left an impact on you. Why would I search for the name "Vanessa Lou or Latasha James" when I come to Youtube to learn about branding or Instagram? Because I know they have something to give me.

Branding is more than what you want me to see or how you want me to see you. Branding is how I see you.
This brings us to "how to brand your page as a creative".

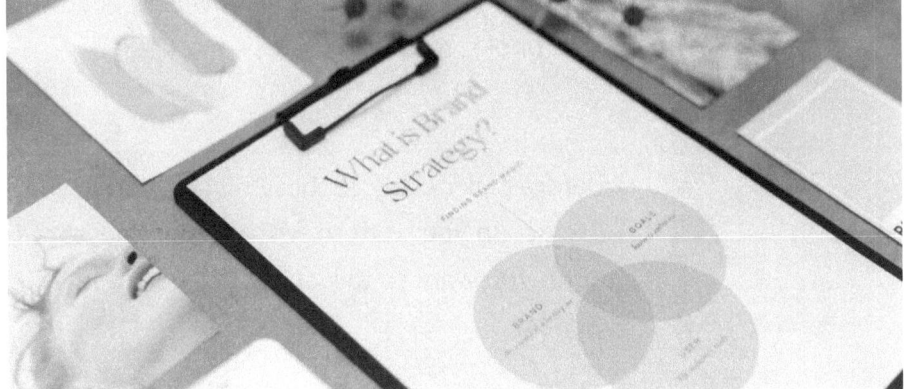

02 How to build a brand as a creative

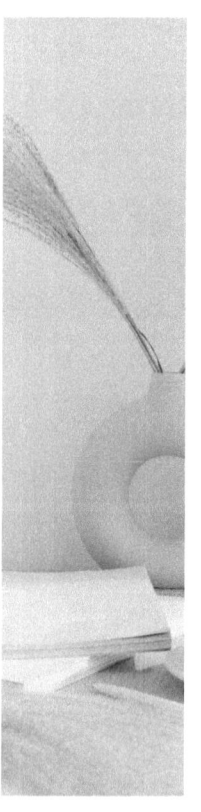

To build a brand, you have to ask and answer these 5 questions
1. What is your brand about?
2. Who is your brand for?
3. Where to find them?
4. How to get to them?
5. How to keep them?

What is your brand about?
This is where we talk about picking a niche but picking a niche is a lot deeper than just picking. We have niches like lifestyle, fashion, beauty, hair, books, movies, business, marketing, creatives e.t.c.

Before picking any of these niches, you have to decide, do you want to write about your content or do you want to talk about your content with videos.

3 people can pick lifestyle as their niche but they do that in different ways with one of them writing about how his day went or what he learned from something that happened in his day while the other uses mini video clips to show you how his day went or what he did in a day without saying a word and the last person creates a video or audio where he talks about his day or what he learned from it.

These 3 people are lifestyle creators, but they talk about lifestyle in different ways. If I want to listen to lifestyle content in an audio form or hear someone talk about life, I go to no 3, if I want to just watch clips of activities around a person's life, I go to no 2 and if I want to read about life, I go to no 1.

Example 2; let's say you pick books or movies as your niche. This niche can go 3 ways. You can be a reviewer, a recommender, or both. Some book pages or movie pages do not review books or movies, they only recommend them. In this case, what is their brand for? What do you go there to get? If you need book recommendations, you go to brand A but if you want to check out the review of a book, you go to brand B.

Some brands do both, but if you want your brand to be known for providing both, you have to maintain an equilibrium between both, ensuring that you don't create more of recommendation content than review content that your brand becomes known for just recommendations.

For example, I followed a movie page because I was looking for Chinese drama recommendations and I saw it in their page. I moved down the page and after about 7 contents, all I saw next were short movie clips. That wasn't what I wanted, it was not what I thought the brand stood for which brought me to the brand that I'm seeing, so I left.

Example 3; On my page, I create lifestyle/story content & Educational and how-to content. I try to make my page a blend of both by having 2 different colors for both. If you see the white color, you know its lifestyle or story content, if you see the brown color, you know it's educational or how-to content. In the same way, you can try maybe using videos for educational content and written carousels for lifestyle content.

This is when you want your brand to be known for 2 different things you want to build a community around 2 different types of content but you want to make it easy for the audience of each type of content to identify.

In choosing more than one niche, you can also combine both niches to serve as one. For example; I picked lifestyle and creatives as my niche. I teach creatives about growing, branding, positioning, and everything in between but I also made my lifestyle about creatives. When I talk about life or my life experience, I make sure it relates to creatives' life or how their life is or how it can affect them.

You can also decide to mix different niches without combining them. For example; books and lifestyle or movies and self-growth e.t.c. just find a balance between both so one niche does not overshadow the other.

Note: Let's say you are a social media manager. You must not create social media management tips. You can decide to focus your brand on providing growth tips for business owners, you can decide to provide tips for creatives as a whole, or you can decide to focus your brand on providing content that is not social media management related.

What you need to find out is what you want your brand to be known for. If you want to be known as a video or audio lifestyle creator or a lifestyle content writer. If you want people to think about book recommendations and think of your brand.

Who is your brand for?
Everybody is not your audience. If your brand niche is books and you focus on book recommendations, what type of books do you recommend? Is it thriller? Romance? Personal growth ? or all types of books? Who should come to your brand? Who do you want in your brand?

For example; my brand niche is creatives, but I narrowed it down to new or newly stuck creatives. I don't want everybody, my brand is not for everybody, it's just for people that want to become creatives, newly became creatives, or became creatives not so long ago but are stuck on what to do with their brand.

Example 2; your brand is about personal growth and well-being. What aspect of it does your brand cover? Is it the mental aspect that helps with confidence, anxiety or the social aspect of the relationship or do you also cover the financial aspect about making money, budgeting, saving, or the spiritual aspect e.t.c all these aspects are things I need for growth but which one is your brand for? which group of people do you want to come to your brand? People, who need help with the mental aspect of personal growth or the social aspect? Or is it the financial aspect?

Example 3; This one involves money and location. If you are building your brand intending to earn, how much is the lowest or highest price you would sell a course or service?

If you are going to sell a course #10,000, then your brand should focus on getting people who can afford and are willing to pay #10,000 for something they see as valuable.

They must not have it immediately, but they should be able to save up that amount of money and be willing to use it to pay for a service or product. At my stage in life, there is an amount of money that I can't use to purchase a service or product. It's not because it's not important or valuable but because I can't afford it. If I'm your brand audience and your product is at that price, then I am not who your brand is for.

This is the same thing for location. For example, your brand is a marketing brand for business owners in Anambra, I am a business owner but I am not in Anambra hence location has become our barrier.

Where to find them & How to get to them?
Now, you know who your brand is for, then how do you get them? Where do you find them? This is the next step. Sometimes, your target audience would not come to you but you have to go and look for them where they already are. You have to go and seek their attention.

For example, if your brand is focused on females, where do you think you can find them? Brands like girlily dotcom would work well for you. You are targeting creatives, have you checked out brands whose target audience is similar to yours and didn't see anything?

When I say going to brands that already have your target audience, I don't mean it in the sense of stealing the audience but in the sense of reaching new people. I'm not saying go and follow all their audience so they can follow back, that mindset would kill your brand before it starts. You having 80 followers and following 2000 people makes your brand look like a scam.

Instead, start engaging with that brand's content, engage with your target audience, comment under the brand's content, and like their comment, they get notifications. Go to their page and engage with their content, like it, and drop meaningful comments. Seek their attention and get them to notice you.

Go to the hashtag your target audience mainly uses and engage with content under it. Check out the contents of your target audience and repost those you resonate with, drop something meaningful about it or how it resonated with you, and tag them to it. Don't overdo this or start tagging them every time you post even when the post does not concern them. You are doing this to let them notice you not for them to feel like you want to use them or gain something from them.

Note, even though the brand has your target audience, your target audience is uniquely yours and there may be a difference. If your price range for your target audience is #50,000, then even if the brand has your target audience, what is the price value of the audience? Is your positioning going to be the same as that brand? What I'm trying to say is that even if they have your audience, all their audience is not yours.

Your content is another way to get your target audience. Create valuable content using a content strategy with your goal in mind (would talk about that further down the book), and make use of hashtags that your target audience would search for.

How to keep them?
To be frank with you, the only thing that can help you keep your audience is providing them with value. But here is the thing, value is different for everybody. To some people, they find value when you share content based on your experience or when you share free tips, or when you share funny or relatable content.

Also, building a strong community is going to help you. You can build a community in two ways:

1. People that love your content, see you as an authority and would love to be associated with you or your brand hence they are always supporting you and your content.
2. People who know they can count on your support hence they support you too.

Note; Community building requires time and effort to not only create valuable content for your brand but to also engage, connect and support the content &brand of others.

But the main thing of all is to maintain the type of content you started with that brought that set of audience. If I started following your brand because you share funny content and then along the line, you start sharing educational content, unless I find value in that kind of content, you have lost me as an Audience, even though I may not unfollow, I may not engage with that content and that's why rebranding is almost like starting afresh.

Let's talk about Rebranding.

03
How to Rebrand

To rebrand, you have to ask yourself a question, why do I want to rebrand? What do I want to change about my brand? Is it my niche? My content? My brand aim? My target audience? What do I want my new brand to be about?

For example; your brand was formerly positioned as a social media manager brand that's focused on providing social media growth tips for business owners, but now you want to become a Canva tutor who shares design & canva tutorials for business owners. You can see that you are changing your brand niche, your brand aim which is to provide social media growth tips, and your content, but your target audience remains the same (business owners).

Note; you can decide to niche down on your target audience according to the tips in the Ebook. Maybe you can decide that instead of all types of business owners, you want to share design & canva tutorials for only fashion or clothing business owners.

Example 2; Let's say you are a content writer and have built a writing brand using lifestyle content but now, you want to rebrand and start creating educational content for writers, you can see that you are not changing the fact that you are a content writer, but you are changing your content and in that line, your target audience is going to change.

Example 3; Let's say you are a content creator for the fashion niche but your brand is not doing as well as you want, and you want to rebrand. You don't want to change your niche or target audience but you want to change your brand positioning. You want people to see your brand as more valuable, you want to build an authority for the brand. Then you know it's time to look at your content. Why is your content not converting? Why is your strategy not working? Is your content as valuable as that of others in your niche? If the answer is no, you need to change the type of content you create. Not in the sense of creating new content that is not fashion content, but tweaking the fashion content you create to be as valuable as those of others in your niche while still adding your unique twist to the content. In this case, you have to do a competitor analysis. What type of content do people in your niche create? Which of the content works the most for them? Which of their content do you enjoy?

When rebranding your page, you can decide on announcing your rebranding to your audience, you can decide on just showing the rebranding with the switch in your content type or you can just let your audience detect the rebranding themselves.

But note that if you are not maintaining the same niche or content type in your rebranding, you may lose followers or have a reduced engagement. This is because you are almost starting afresh and as such you might need a new target audience since maybe your present audience is no longer your target audience now. This is also where your community comes into play. If you have built a strong community, most of them might stick with you.

04 How to build a valuable brand

When you hear a "valuable brand", what comes to your mind? A brand you can get something from right? A brand that can provide you with answers to your problem right? And that should be what you aim to achieve with your brand if you want to build a valuable brand.

There are a lot of brands in your niche and they all upload content but what makes your content different? What type of content do you need to start creating that would make people feel like you can help them when they have a problem related to your niche?

There are contents called "googleable content" .

This is content that can be easily found when you search on google. And you should know that if you can easily get that content, others can too.

When creating a valuable brand, you have to think outside the box. Even if you get your content ideas from google, how do you modify them to give them that unique human touch? Do you copy verbatim from google?

The best content to build a valuable brand is from experience. Share what you know, share what you have overcome, share what you feel, share what you see, and be creative because that's what makes your content unique and provides a value only you can give.

To create a valuable brand, you have to be ready to share value for free.

There are some brands you come to and when you see their content, you are like if they share this much for free, what would they share during their paid session? And that's what makes them valuable to you, that's what makes you trust that they can deliver and that's what makes them an authority in their niche to you.

Be ready to share VALUE for free, that's what makes you a VALUABLE BRAND.

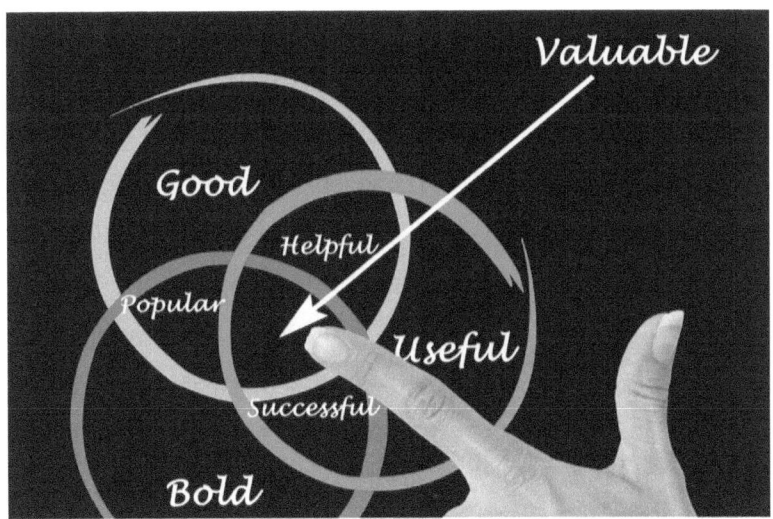

05 How to build a consistent brand

Building a consistent brand involves more than just posting every day or thrice a week. It also reflects in your content.

For example your brand content is usually about growth tips for business owners, but suddenly, you are posting motivational quotes all the time. Yes, motivational and inspirational contents are a type of content you can also post, but is that what your brand is focused on? Why would business owners who come to your brand to get tips to grow all of a sudden, they are seeing motivational content everywhere.

Is that what they came for? one or two motivational content is not bad, but making it your brand's main content may start hinting at the fact that you are rebranding even if you are not and this would lead to the loss of some audience.

When creating content for your brand, ask yourself questions like is this content in line with my brand's goal? Would my audience appreciate this type of content? Does this content align with my brand? Don't just create content and upload it just so your page would be active, remember that you have people that would receive that content. How would they receive it? Will it be valuable to them? Put that into consideration.

When it comes to staying consistent in terms of posting schedule, 3 things can help you but first, you have to decide on your posting frequency. Do you want to post daily? Every 2 days? 3 times a day? 3 times a week?

You have to first decide on this and then move to the three things
i. Content calendar creation
ii. Content repurposing
iii. Content scheduling

Content calendar creation
In creating your content calendar, you need to put certain things into consideration and two of them are who are you serving? What are you serving? This would help you decide on the next thing and that is your CONTENT PILLAR. Your content pillars are the things your content revolves around and these are decided by your audience.

For example my brand's target audience is creatives and not just creatives, Instagram creatives, what type of content do I want to serve or do I serve them? Instagram growth tips, Instagram branding tips.

This would help me decide on my content pillar which are creatives, Instagram creatives, Instagram growth tips for creatives, branding tips for creatives, and Instagram branding tips for creatives.

Having this content pillar and creating content around it would ensure that my content is consistently in line with my branding, brand goals, and positioning. Note that your content pillar may change in line with different activities your brand is undergoing at that moment.

For example: if I want to promote a digital product I'm selling, my content pillar may or may not include providing growth tips or branding tips, instead, it may change to complement what I'm selling and why you should buy it.

E.g if it's a consultation service I want to promote, I may add consultation for creatives, or paid service to my content pillar so I can source content like the benefits of consultations, the difference between paid services & free services, and What you would get from my consultation service e.t.c.

After getting your content pillar down, it's time to write down the different types of content so you can get a mix of all of them for your brand.

Let's talk about the content types:

1. Educational content; this is content that educates your audience about something. It helps you build authority as an expert because you are teaching and impacting value. E.g How to be consistent in creating content as a creative.
2. Problem-solving content: this is almost the same as educational content but instead of teaching a broad topic like educational content, this type of content focuses on just one point. E.g how to be consistent in creating content as a creative includes creating a content calendar, content repurposing & content scheduling this is for educational content. When it's problem-solving content, you can decide to pick just a content calendar and give a detailed description of how to create a content calendar with all the necessary steps and strategies. In this type of content, you are picking one point from a bunch and going further to dissect it to solve a problem. You can use both educational & problem-solving content together, I just prefer differentiating it.

1. Inspirational/ motivational content: this is content that inspires and motivates people to do something. It can be content that inspires confidence, inspires time management, inspires or motivates people to believe in their dreams e.t.c. This can be in the form of a personal story, a quote e.t.c. This type of content also helps your audience to relate with you.
2. Relatable content: this is content your audience can relate to. Either based on things that happen in their life, job, environment, the situation of the country e.t.c. For example: for my page that is focused on creatives, I can talk about pricing, finding clients, and problems with maintaining consistency. A book blogger can talk about the hike in the prices of books, TBR list e.t.c. a lifestyle creative can talk about life in general from money issues, to love to self-care e.t.c. Relatable content is one type of content that can get people's attention because it resonates with them.

1. Trust-building content: This is content used to build trust with your audience. It can be reviews, snippets of your work or you working, a picture or video of your workspace or equipment e.t.c.
2. Promotional content; This is content used to promote a service or product. It can be full-blown promotional content like a carousel or video of your services or product, it can also be light promotion like you creating content about a particular problem of your audience and then referring them to your service or product as the solution to the problem.

After listing out the types of content, you can then create contents that encompass these different types of content using your content pillar as a guideline for content topics or direction.

Note that you must not use all the different types of content, I sometimes don't use them all when planning my content calendar for the month.

You can plan your content calendar using tools like Google Sheets, Google Docs, Asana, Airtable, and Notion. I think the Canva app has a content calendar planner although I haven't used it. You can check out Youtube for tutorials.

Content repurposing
This involves using my content in different forms or for different platforms. If you use more than one platform, this is the one for you.

You can repurpose Instagram reels to Tiktok videos & Youtube shorts, repurpose your Youtube sit-down educational video to a Blog post (I have done this about 2 times), your Newsletter to an Instagram Carousel post or a LinkedIn post, Your newsletter title/topic to an Instagram quote reel or Twitter tweet (if it can say something on its own), highlight the main points of your youtube long educational video and use it as an Instagram reel or single post.

You can also use the content you create on one platform as your content for the day on another platform. For example: from January to May, the second Sunday and last Sunday of the month, the content that is planned for my page is announcing my new blog post because these are the days I upload blogs.
This helps me in advertising my blog post, but it also helps me in consistency and provides me with content to post on my Instagram for those two days.

This is similar to Youtubers who post Jpegs of their video or thumbnail or a short clip of their video on their feed as the post for that day.

Content scheduling
This helps to ensure that you show up on your feed even if you are busy or indisposed. You can schedule your Facebook & Instagram posts using Meta Business Suite but you must have a Facebook page. You can use the Preview app but I think it's a paid app. For Youtube & Tiktok, you can schedule them directly on their respective apps. Instagram reels could not be scheduled before, but I saw an update on an Instagram page @latermedia which I think is a scheduling & publishing platform announcing that Instagram reels can be auto-published on their platform, so you can check that out.

When you have put all this into place, maintaining a consistent brand won't be so hard.

06

How to monetize your brand

―――――――

You can monetize your brand in different ways. From services you offer to influencing or Ads to Digital products or classes.

Monetizing your brand successfully with a digital product, class or webinar depends on understanding what your brand is known for, what you have built authority with, what your audience comes to your page for, and what kind of questions you have been asked.

For example, my brand is focused on creatives, but I'm also a content writer &Content storyteller and I've been asked questions on branding, content writing & storytelling, growth tips e.t.c. Hence, if I'm monetizing my brand with a digital product or class, I'm looking towards creating an Ebook on branding or growth tips for creatives, hosting a class on it, or teaching about how to become a content writer or storyteller, or starting a consultation class on it.

Even if you feel you don't have anything deep to teach, do you know that people would pay to learn how to begin?

The first ebook I wrote was an ebook on social media growth (Instagram, Facebook & Whatsapp) for beginners.

You can do the same. You are a student and a blogger? You can write an ebook on how you started your blog as a student, the processes of setting up your blog, the people or resources you used, how you maintained a balance between school & blogging, and if you have started earning from it, you can add how you do that and if there are other benefits you get from blogging, you can add that too.

You are a content creator and always get asked how you maintain a beautiful feed aesthetic or how you take your pictures or videos or how you edit them.You can create a preset, you can write a short ebook on how you became a content creator, how you earn from it, or just how you maintain your page aesthetics, how you take & edit your pictures and videos e.t.c. you can decide to make it a combo pack and sell the preset along with the aesthetic ebook.

You are a student and a successful business owner. You can write a beginner Ebook for students who want to start running a business based on your experience, tell us how you started, how you choose your business, how you maintain a balance between both e.t.c.

You successfully made a transition from one job niche to another or you successfully finished a rebranding of your brand that worked in your favor. You can write a short beginner ebook for others who also want to do that but don't know how to. Teach them with your experience so they make fewer mistakes.

You are a social media manager but your page is focused on growth tips for business owners or you are a graphic designer and you are very good at canva design, curate that knowledge into an ebook for business owners' growth or a class or course on canva design.

You are a travel blogger, fashion blogger, or food blogger. As a travel blogger, You can curate an ebook on how to holiday in Dubai with $1000 if that is how much you used. Give me a list of where you stayed, how to book them, how much you spent, where you visited, how you processed your document e.t.c. anything to make my journey easier.

As a fashion blogger, you can curate an ebook that helps me color match outfits, tells me the type of outfit for each occasion, helps me with styling outfits, and teaches me how to be a fashion blogger. As a food blogger, you can curate an Ebook on places to eat that are aesthetically pleasing that a content creator would love.

If you have good knowledge of how to grow on another platform, you can curate a book or service on that. E.g how to grow on Pinterest, how to grow on Youtube, Tiktok, Linkedin e.t.c.

Know that people are ready to buy your story if they see its benefit in your life and feel like it would benefit them too.

Note: your pricing can also be affected by your brand positioning. I know we all want to charge $20 for the sales of one Ebook, but from the positioning of your brand does your audience think that your book or your service is worth that price? Do they feel the value they would get from that product is worth the price you are charging? How you position your brand and the value your audience feels your brand can offer matters.

I'm not saying you should undercharge but put a reasonable price based on not only the value of the book but also the perception people have of your brand. You can take the first book as a show of your authority. If it's value-packed then people are seeing you as an Authority and selling the second book at a higher price would be easier. Everything happens in stages.

07 Content strategy

A content strategy is simply how you use your content to achieve a goal you have for the content. I'm going to be using myself as an example. You can create a content strategy using three things:
1. Content Format
2. Content-type
3. Content

Content Format
From January to April, I was creating Flat Lay picture posts with most of my content in my caption and I noticed that I was getting comments, but I wasn't getting as many shares and saves as I wanted.

I looked around and noticed that carousel and tweet-like posts were getting more shares and save so I switched to creating that format of content. I used it in May & June and it achieved what I wanted from it(more shares &saves). Now this July, I want more reach and although some people's carousels do have high reach, mine doesn't have very high reach so this month, I want to use more reels.

Content type
If you want your content to be focused on making sales, you can use the promotional type of content. If you want it to get you more comments or shares, you can try relatable or motivational content because a lot of people relate to that type of content. If you want it to get you more shares, try educational or problem-solving content because people love free value and love to learn new things.

Content

If you want to bring your content to the face of a new niche of people e.g you are a lifestyle content writer but you want bookstagrammers to notice your content, you can create content bookstagrammers can relate to and then maybe add a CTA-like tag the bookstagrammers you know. If you want more people to engage with your content, you can create content that allows you to tag people or refer to people. When you tag people for things that they feel are relevant to them, they usually engage and reply to your tag.

"Finally, just take your branding one step at a time and your dream brand would surely come to fulfillment."

Drop your review of the ebook here, I would appreciate it.

Conclusion and Next Steps

If you need to ask me any questions, you can DM me on Instagram.

I also offer a paid 1:1 consultation session for creatives. You can chat me up on Instagram to book a slot. You can also check out my Selar shop to buy any of my first 2 short Ebooks and use the discount code SOCIAL MEDIA & CONTENT respectively to get 10% off each of them when you purchase.

[SELAR SHOP](#)

THANK YOU for your Purchase.

I hope this Ebook taught you a thing or two and I hope you put it into practice and build the brand of your dream.

Igwilo chinenye sincere

www.ingramcontent.com/pod-product-compliance
Lightning Source LLC
Chambersburg PA
CBHW031532210526
45464CB00020B/2824